PRAISE FOR ***SEARCHING FOR PETCO***

In Skylar Alexander's *Searching for Petco*, a coming-of-age story unfolds in reverse: first we meet a sardonically self-aware millennial who knows the ways she's let her identity become monetized and boxed into 140 characters, but is too savvy to stop side-hustling. Searching for something beyond commodified selfhood, she becomes an avatar-heroine of video games and pure imagination, insisting that real desire might yet exist beyond all the scripts of digital culture, the gig economy, and gender. She's desirous in a way a woman isn't supposed to be, repeating "I want, I want, I want" even as she confronts sexual violence with guns strapped to her heels. Try as she might to guard her heart, she can't, and so she crashes through to her roots, arriving at the rusted-out Midwestern river town hiding inside "the cellar door / of [her] ribcage," driving around lost, searching for Petco. Amidst urban ruins, family ghosts, and dried-up pensions, she never locates the store or the person she used to be, but instead affirms that she always was who she is—the knowing that hurls so many artists out of the nest. In this gutsy, acrobatic, and heartfelt first collection, using innovative forms that dazzle the eye and ear, Alexander's voice of her generation reaches us—"we American trashcans full of unfilterable noise"—by ringing out too urgently to ignore.

—Becca Klaver, author of *Empire Wasted* and *Ready for the World*

In *Searching for Petco*, Skylar Alexander creates spaces to explore devastating tragedy alongside everyday concerns, and she does so with fluid ingenuity in both form and language, yet the language has a precise directness to it that often startles the reader into moments of profound clarity. And throughout the book, there's a tantalizing propulsion with which we speed down the halls of, say, millennialness (is that even a word?), and along the way we glimpse portraits of humor, insight, and an undercurrent of frustration, even anger. And truth. Always truth. Alexander's voice is urgent, candid, and much needed. *Searching for Petco* is a startling and memorable debut.

—Keith Lesmeister, author of *We Could Have Been Happy Here*

Skylar Alexander's *Searching for Petco* is a restless, fearless debut collection. 'A harvesting of halos', these poems are myth-making and myth-dismantling: seeking, out of the materials of the present, a new kind of holiness. We must 'go slow / and see the damage / or the damage will take you'. Alexander writes into the damage to wrest solace from the modern dislocation and loss of self: not by rejecting the modern, but by taking up the masks it offers and making them speak a fresh, troubling, and beautiful language. *Searching for Petco* is an urgent, feverous, and brilliant debut from a poet to be followed.

—Chad Campbell, author of *Laws & Locks* and *Nectarine*

Searching for Petco is a mutant blast radius of righteous Midwestern anger and tender observation: Alexander takes a fire axe to our tech-bound, corporate-branded culture, wrecks misogyny and patriarchy with a fire axe, and turns hashtags into piercing poetic jabs. These poems are for all of us frustrated citizens searching for hope in the cruelty and gracelessness, all of us running errands, looking for a store in a strip mall, but finding a river, a sky, a friend instead.

—Adam Fell, author of *Dear Corporation* and *I Am Not A Pioneer*

Furious, on fire, and achingly caustic, these poems tear through the page as you read, searching for a moment of rest in a reckless world, a moment where, like "the lava of my body | turning | there's a Shinto god," verse might fuse frustration into insight. This book is a wild ride through that heroic quest.

—Lauren Haldeman, author of *Instead of Dying* and *Calenday*

SEARCHING FOR
PETCO

SEARCHING FOR PETCO

POEMS BY

SKYLAR ALEXANDER

FORKLIFT_BOOKS

FORKLIFT BOOKS EDITION, JANUARY 2022

ISBN 978-0-9995931-9-6

Edited by Matt Hart
Book and cover design by Eric Appleby

Body text is set in Skolar Latin
Titles are set in Acumen Pro Semi-Condensed
Nothing is set in Stone.

FORKLIFT_BOOKS
Cincinnati, Ohio
WWW.FORKLIFTBOOKS.COM

SEARCHING FOR...

SEARCHING FOR
PETCO

HOW ARE YOU FEELING TODAY?

Today I am *Love is Just Around the Corner*
Today I am *Love is Gonna Save Us*
Today I am *Love Will Tear Us Apart*
Today I am *Love is a Losing Game*
Today I am *Crazy in Love*
Today I am *Love, in Itself*
Today I am *A List of Demands*
Today I am *We're Going to Be Friends*
Today I am *Just Friends*
Today I am *Zero*
Today I am *Please Call Me, Baby*
Today I am *Wish You Were Here*
Today I am *All Apologies*
Today I am *Bullet Proof... I Wish I Was*
Today I am *Bullet with Butterfly Wings*
Today I am *Burnin' and Lootin'*
Today I am *Search and Destroy*
Today I am *Renegade*
Today I am *Death to Everyone*
Today I am *Dead*
Today I am *Orpheus in the Underworld*

Today I am *Whistlin' Past the Graveyard*
Today I am *The Wicked Messenger*
Today I am *Witchy Woman*
Today I am *Sorcerer*
Today I am *Santeria*
Today I am *Asking For It*
Today I am *Date Rape*
Today I am *Hit Me*
Today I am *Hit the Road Jack*
Today I am *Weak and Powerless*
Today I am *Oh My Golly!*
Today I am *Oh No!*
Today I am *Survivor*
Today I am *Time Bomb*
Today I am *Another Brick in the Wall*
Today I am *A Horse with No Name*
Today I am *Minnie the Moocher*
Today I am *Lovely Rita*
Today I am *Miss America*
Today I am *New Born*
Today I am *A New Kind of Army*
Today I am *What the World Needs Now*
Today I am *The New Year*
Today I am *Say My Name*
Today I am *Just a Girl*

MY NAME IS MILLENNIAL, AND I'M NOT OKAY

My name is Millennial, and I'm not okay.
I'm a Capital C Creative; I side hustle
like a motherfucker; I'm fluent
in Adobe and I got all kinds
of artistic hobbies.

Let me tell you—
this here is a girl who knows
her way around Mod Podge
and a power sander! No really,
check my blog—
here's my card
yes, letter pressed—
no, it's okay,
be impressed;
the ink costs more
than human blood.

My name is Millennial, and I'm not okay.
Today, my intention is to not burn myself
just because I'm burning out—
like my porch all full of shit-bags flaming
like Amelia Earhart crashing into the ocean flaming
like this volleyball is my only friend flaming
like a *STOP, DROP & ROLL* PSA flaming
like a Sim with no cooking skills making Goopy
        Carbonara flaming
like I got a whole house of aloe plants for these sick
        burns flaming—
and aren't they really sick?
Man am I sick
with these burns!

My name is Millennial, and I'm not okay.
Every day I greet this flaming world
cool as a cucumber—
like I WEAR MY SUNGLASSES AT NIGHT cool
like THE FUTURE IS SO BRIGHT I GOTTA WEAR
        SHADES cool
like break out the SHUTTER SHADES and Kanye's
        STRONGER
and let's party like it's not problematic—
Every day is #tbt for me!

My name is Millennial, and I'm not okay.
Check me on Instagram, looking so
NAMASTE, BITCHES
#sofire #solit #sowoke

My name is Millennial, and I'm not okay.
#iwokeuplikethis #typeababe #weekendwarrior
#jk #namastayinbed #sundaypunday #thatmillenniallife
#technologydetox #smartphoneclense #jk
#thatmillenniallife #nofilter #sofire #onfire
#thisisfine #letskeepgoing #soitogoes

My name is Millennial, and I'm not okay.
Let me be your roadmap to trending
look at me going viral—
#youlikemeyoureallylikeme #sallyfield
#mrsdoubtfiretheswansongofmygeneration

You see, I got it down to a science—
I'm a #hashtagscientist like that:
combine one part #politicalcommentary
with equal parts #90snostalgia; blend
#shakennotstirred; garnish with #trendinghashtags
I call your cocktail #hashtagactivism
I call your cocktail #avocadotoast

I call your cocktail #killingthediamondindustry
I call your cocktail #kettleblack
I call your cocktail #whatitis
I call your cocktail #metoo

#metoo #methree #mefour
We out here #hashtaggingforpeace
#hashtaggingforserenity #hashtaggingformeaning
A koan in 140 characters or less:
#whatisthesoundofonehandclapping
#howdoyougetthroughthegatelessgate
#whatisblackandwhiteandreadallover
#kierkegaardanddogenwalkintoabar
#spoileralert #thegirldiesattheend

I AM ALWAYS BOILING WITH A SENSE OF BLOOD & GUTS I AM TOO VEGAN TO UNDERSTAND

5 o'clock and I'm fighting
the urge to veer wildly
into oncoming traffic—
to take up the katana
that lives in my backseat and go
full death god on these suburbanites
and their minivans and their
MAGA bumper stickers

here you are:
a human animal, cornered
in a labyrinth of skyscrapers
and annual reports;
you don't even look up
when walking anymore
but please—
tell me more about how you really feel;
tell me how you really made a mess of things,

but please—
I only speak in #hashtags
140 characters or bust

you and I
we are hungry ghosts,
always in want of;
insatiable friend, let's not
pretend to be profound
in our wanting

I want to rip my own throat out,
but even so, I refuse
to sleep in the Bat Cave;
each day a battle to keep
my flamethrower breath in check;
I'm a Klingon, growing tired
and old, hungry for battle—
for an honorable death

on the day of your death,
foretell the self-help books
to which I've entrusted my life,
you will not be judged
by the number of coffees you drank,

the money you tithed,
the birthdays you forgot, remembered,
then forgot again, nor
the statuettes erected to worship
your every selfie saved;

when you finally
kick the bucket
you will be judged
by the taste you've left
in the mouths of
the ones who loved you—
in the sneeze of good
your blink of life
allowed you to do

they say you get the life you choose
to live, so choose well

they say, make your own daily bread—
let the yeast rise, make caverns winding,

they say, employ a map, find the treasures buried
inside yourself; strip mine your mountains,
franchise yourself; blog about it

ELEGY FOR IPHONE

She has risen—
My iPhone an Old Testament God; unfeeling,
she deletes people indiscriminately. She floods
the world with her indifference, her many plagues
erasing connections, entire relationships, a life in texts—
razed to fragments, then fragments gone.

She has risen—
My iPhone the forbidden fruit, and I, Eve,
wishing to Wikipedia every little thing—
burning thirst for morseled truth
turning ash in my long, thin throat.

She has risen—
My iPhone an oracle; she knows
I don't need to know what makes
construction paper different from
ordinary paper at 2:30 in the morning.
She knows knowledge alone won't bring back
those red threads I've lost to death.

She has risen—
My iPhone a Zen priestess
exorcising evil—the emails
I obsessively re-read before falling asleep
If I touch anything, gone. She doesn't respond
to my touch anymore. She listens
to my prayers, but she doesn't speak
my language any longer. I shout
Call Grandma into oblivion.
Only cicadas. Only *I can't find Barbara in your contacts.*
Would you like me to search for locations with that name?

RORSCHACH

this morning | all fired up |
with speed | believing in fad |
for adrenaline | like insulin |
this hearthheart |

blood and guts | this morning |
tomorrow | I love |
yellow hyphen to Nazca line |
I'll soar a firebird | I'll tirefire immortal |
I'm desperate | this morning | to

to become | an archipelago |
to land in the water | in my heart |
for you | I'll dance | I'll fog | I'll campfire |

this morning | the smog thick |
in Canada |
so south | as to be seen |

this morning | I am small and weak |
a rabbit ensnared | thrashing
sandpaper | this wool itch

TEST

| this morning | fucked up | with fervor
| in AS SEEN ON TV | as in | this desire
| as in | this boiling
| this sense of

| I love | the barracuda in the water
| the lurch of | speed metal blurring
| but | this morning
| I'll holyroller tongue | if it'll help
fracture | to become | this morning

| of thought | the lava of my body | turning
| there's a Shinto god | speaking to you
| for you | if it'll help

| they say it's fires | run wild
| last week | the northern lights dipped
| in Midwestern driveways

| this morning | this world makes me
death thrashes | this world makes | my sand
of breathing | in | out | in again

ROZENGURTLE BAUMGARTNER, UNTOUCHED BY MAN

Today I am that woman in *The Boondock Saints*
who is sucker-punched by Norman Reedus
for explaining to the viewer
that our everyday language
betrays a dark history—
that every casual "rule of thumb"
forgets the woman purpled by it;
I am the man charismatic
in my apron bloody, quipping, *Perhaps*
it shoulda been the rule of wrist. Ha!; I am a riot
in the meat packing plant;
I am a good laugh, riotous;
I am a bloody prank between brothers, my face
redwet with the slap of tongues, over

and over; redwet, I am what's left
on the cutting room floor: a joke
How many feminists does it take to screw in a light bulb?
Beat. *Two. One ta screw it in and one ta suck my cock!;*

I am what you see on screen: *oh, come on*
it's St. Patty's Day! It's all in good fun;
I am a bloodletting, a celluloid cutting
to make McManus brothers read sympathetic; today,

I am every woman still hot for Norman Reedus despite
those early-career punches; I am the whole bloody cult
of Daryl Dixon, the social media missus,
née every woman seeking a Real Man
to protect her from the other Real Men,
née my Man is Different, née He Will Be
Different with Me; nay, despite

all these years of progress, here I am—Roz Baumgartner,
still a woman-parrot; still a woman reduced
to flannelled stereotype, yet still a woman trying
to eek out a life; this all another way of saying
I am still the woman hot for the man who sucker-
        punches her;
I am still the woman with meat shoved in her face,
slapped, over, and over; the sucker
punched; the punchline; *Ha! Ba-dum-bum TISH!*

BAYONETTA

I want to be a woman in the way Bayonetta is a woman,
which is to say, I want to be a caricature of a woman;
which is to say, I want to be burlesque and absurd
I want to trade
in my hymns for swords;
my LPs for lollipops;
I want to make everything sexy; I want to weaponize
my hair; to strap guns to my heels when I perform
my miracles of contortion; to name them
Cult of Domesticity and *Here I Stand Ironing,*
and I want all the bad guys to notice me;
I want to harvest their halos—
trophies to relive the moment
of their execution.

I want to be a woman
of varied gameplay; equal parts dungeon
crawler and arcade; chase and brawl

I want to have something
for everyone;
I want to be fun
for the whole family, that is,
so long as the family is old enough
to get past my ESRB rating;
I want to be a satisfying experience
you reflect on and think,
>> *replay value* <<
I want to embody everything
God hates in a woman, and then
I want to strangle God
with my thighs
like I learned in my jiu-jitsu class;

I want my pussy
to be the last thing the bad guys see
before the quick time event, the cutscene;
I want the sniveling
video game critics to see me and think,
Lara Croft without the British prudishness;
I want them to think
my kind of woman;

I want to do so well
in the international market
that I come back for a sequel, liberated
from my catsuit of hair;
I want to be a title that anchors a system
in a competitive marketplace;
I want to be farmed out;

I want to penetrate and disseminate;

I want to become so popular
that it becomes uncool to like me;

I want to take the idea of me
and run with it so hard I run
right off the cliff.

CONFESSION

For once, I want to be honest,
& I want it to be for real—
face to face, not folded
into this purpled bullshit—
the scaffolding of another
crypt keeper poem.

I want to gather up
my loved ones—
I want to unhinge
the cellar door
of my ribcage & reveal
my cobwebbed truths,
strategically buried
to act as the foundation
of my withheld convictions.

Most of all
I want my loved ones
to smile, say, *Fucker,*

like that's been a secret.
Little Shit, like we didn't know—
like we care about any of that,
& together we'll kindle up
a blaze, burn shit, & get sloshed

& suddenly it's Easter dinner—
same spiral ham, same corn casserole, but
everybody's got a Keystone and
something nice to say, & even
teetotaler grandma will put down
the Bible for a minute, unclip
her clip-on earrings, unclutch
her pearls & breathe

If worst comes to worst, I want
the strength to hold the ones I love
underwater & drown them
like a sack of kittens—
to double-tap & not blink.

If they're to be scathe & scald
in the face of my heart,
I want to be the Mountain, unmoved
by even Icarus crashing to earth.

If it’s to be like this, I want
a No Holds Barred street fight
in a cage of chickenwire where
I will emerge as king of the ring
with a belt that says CHAMPION
& the crowd will love me; the crowd
will storm the stage like I’m Daniel Bryant,
cheering, YES! YES! YES!

MICK FOLEY DEATH WISH

Listen,
I want to rewrite myself to be more
like the many-colored coats I wear;
it should be easy since I don't believe
in a soul, or any unchanging sense
of self anyway.

Listen,
I want to love and not give in
to despair, but
every day I'm despairing.
All I can do is sneeze and hope
it's because someone's thinking of me.

God—
give me the strength
to channel my agony
into something productive,
like getting skinny
or writing grants to the NEA.

Listen,
I want to get to the point
where I don't need to
write poems to live—
where I don't have to
wrestle always with this
oiled menace
lurking in my chest.

Listen,
I got to find an Iggy Pop
Lust for Life at a garage sale
that no one's using. *Yeah,*
I'm through sleeping on the sidewalk
Beating my brains
with the liquor and drugs...

God—
it'd be nice to be immortal
like Mick Foley, but
I'd have to have
a Mick Foley Death Wish—
a Mick Foley Courage to leap
from the top of my cage
and walk away.

Listen,
find me in the dark
a forgotten dustbunny
all graywash ghostly
not yet fleshed out
in color.

Listen,
the birds are singing.
I should be sleeping, but
I'm awake.

God—
I'm sorry, I can't put on the face
that makes the small talk.

THE UNICORN

1.

You meet the unicorn at a bar where you know no one will find you. You stare at the unicorn because you don't know how not to stare at the unicorn. Even the man in the dress stares at the unicorn, but the unicorn doesn't seem to notice. The unicorn stares at you. The unicorn thinks you're a fair maiden, even though your face is masked with blood. You are not a fair maiden, but rather a plague. You do not know how to tell the unicorn this. Who are you to tell the unicorn anything?

2.

At the party for the Malaysian, you see the unicorn holding an alien baby. Everyone at the party is an installation artist or a political revolutionary or a unicorn or you. The unicorn smells you everywhere, calls you lily of the valley when you're really everything and nothing. You and the unicorn walk home, carrying alien babies. When you get home, the unicorn lays their head in your lap and weeps, and you run your fingers through its rainbow mane.

3.

You don't know how your life grew to contain a unicorn, but here you are, at the grocery store with the unicorn; at the DMV with the unicorn; at the climate action rally with the unicorn. You and the unicorn watch *The Last Unicorn* together. You're afraid of the Red Bull, but the unicorn protects you from being driven into the sea. The unicorn is good to you. You try and try to love the unicorn, but you've never loved a unicorn before. You think about the particulars before the feelings; how do you tell your parents you love the unicorn if you can't even tell them you voted Democrat in the last election? They find the mark of the unicorn on your body, and the shame you feel grows into a date palm in your heart.

4.

The unicorn leads you into the tall prairie. The hill is steep, but the unicorn is graceful, picks the path like a mapmaker. The unicorn sees many bats, but you only hear them chirping. The unicorn shines like an opal in the dull, dead grass. The unicorn lets you touch its horn, and you suddenly are a fair maiden, virgin again. The unicorn kisses you and kisses you and kisses you until you're at last shameless.

MAKING CHLORAMINE GAS IN GRANDMA'S BASEMENT

It's easy for me
to believe love
is all around
for I am a sword,
wrapped tight
in a sheath
of onion flesh

If the stars were tomorrow,
the moon a sliver of Cleveland,
& the sun the heir
to my indifference,
I would say
my most difficult muse
is breathing chloramine
vapors in Grandma's
basement

I confess: I am lost

I have made poison
& breathed it deep,
have mammoth-heaved
night to milkmorning,
seeped in sweat
and lemon water

New & all abloom, I rain
my cancered tongue
into the searing raise
of Chicago's skyscrapers;
I gurgle and age &
the base rent of my
1 BR/2 BA/3-piece suit
fits better every year

Every year I'm less
lightning
& kimono,
more jargon
& cinnamon roll

Grandma, tell me,
what is a year of anticlimax
when there's sweet bread
cooling on the windowsill?

Watch: I will evaporate;
become toilet bowl
bleached clean

Watch: I will vaporize;
become ammonia
lighter than air

ascend

GEOSMINA. ORIOL ANGRILL JORDA. 2012.

woman   made of air

you are trace metal &

exhales of

all those who came before you

you got your hair

up in a twist   your cheeks

contoured

like a muscle car   Marinetti

warned us about you

Marinetti welcomed you

with open arms

with arms   marionetted

embrace

cloaked with   cumulonimbus

contort

the fog in the valley   creeps

and you must

through the underbrush

dance   until the sun

burns you away

HERE COMES YOUR MAN

You are *Mighty, Mighty Man*
You are *Rocket Man*
You are *The Man From Harlem*
You are *The Man Who Sold His Beard*
You are *The Man Who Sold the World*
You are *Mr. Magic (Through the Smoke)*
You are *Mr. Grieves*
You are *Mr. November*
You are *Mr. Roboto*
You are *Not a Robot, But a Ghost*
You are *Not the Sun*
You are *Not Sorry*
You are *Not Gonna Get Us*

You are *The Last Man*
You are *The Rifle's Spiral*
You are *Milk and Honey*
You are *Mother*
You are *Most Aborted Father*
You are *My Brother the Gun*

You are *My Iron Lung*
You are *The Wolf at the Door*

You are *In the Hidden Places*
You are *Here, There, Everywhere*
You are *The Air Near My Fingers*
You are *The Hand That Feeds*
You are *The Devil in Mexico*
You are *The Unforgiven*
You are *The Short Way Home*
You are *Gone for Good*

FROM THE SOLAR PLEXUS:

I am the state
of the union
addressing you in my pretty
red dress
with my lips of flame
I fly   I fire
my ray gun buzzing
with mistake
all intergalactic and beastly
a boy wonder
embracing
the parapet
the axe

o leering litany
of complications:
my teeth full of moon
my mother's braided hair
swaying pendulum
arising and falling like breath

in the lung pockmarked
by too many years of factory
like my father the ouroboros
eating his old self
to become new
roots in my braid—
fine and intricate
like the boy who sells beer at John's Grocery
who teaches me to pretend
Schlitz is champagne
Skyrim is caviar
that I wanted this

#NETFLIXANDCHILL

When the man who raped me came to my place
of work asking for my Netflix password, I admit
I could've handled it differently. It had been eleven months
since it happened and we'd not spoken since
his wife and son had come from [REDACTED]
to join him, but he had little money
and I had lots of pity so I let him sponge from me
despite what he did that night when I told him
I didn't want it—see Switch from *The Matrix*,
on her knees looking up, whispering,
not like this, not like this, over and over—not the way he did it
with his wife, but I guess he missed her, or I guess
it didn't matter to him if she didn't want it either.
I told security not to ban him from the hospital
because of his son; it was because of his son

I, the Bride, had allowed him to keep his wicked life
and my Netflix account, but he had become greedy
and took more from me than he should have—
doublefisting *The Vampire Diaries*
on his cellphone and laptop simultaneously
so much that the other parasites on my account
had called to complain. That's the kind of person I am—
unable to get angry enough to do something
to inconvenience my rapist until after he came
not in-between me and my *Househunters International*
        marathon, but
some other person's *Househunters International*
        marathon.
Oprah had told me that a new day was coming—one
where I didn't have to share my Netflix account
with the person who violated me. Tarana Burke told me later,
Girl, take care of yourself. Find others who feel you
and keep fighting. So my question to you, [REDACTED]
Are you still watching? Your time is up.

PERMISSION

"Consent is not a contract but permission
to feel safe among each other"

—Sophia Terezawa

Permission to speak freely. Permission to geek freely, to sleek freely, to fleek freely, to be, freely. Permission to speak falsely. Permission to live in the horse's mouth for fear of any confusion, to fear any confusion of truth. Permission to protest, to picket, to white picket fence (even I have American Dreams). Permission to eat the persimmon in the ice box, so sweet, so cold. Permission to be an icebox and a spitfire, to be the little engine that could. Permission to Google. Permission to not know every answer to every question the schoolboys ask. Permission to crawl before the sun god, the land god, the water god, the TV god, the mocha latte god, the god of Earth, Wind and Fire, the money god, the gun god, the kaleidoscope god, the baby god, the god of brains. Permission to ask. Permission to bask. Permission to pray to the God I don't believe in for fear of believing in nothing. Permission to parse, to pace, to ingratiate myself. Permission to not ingratiate myself. Permission to do nothing. Permission to be holy. Permission to be a temple to whom all others will pray. Permission to be burned, to be looted for the gold I contain. Permission to be frightened. Permission to frighten. Permission to puff up and feather, to peacock, to tell Paul Bunyan tall tales of my own greatness. Permission to protect myself. Permission to promise, to break promise, to break bread, to break down sobbing in the bathtub. Permission to hate this yellow house. Permission to still love despite how poorly I do it. Permission to do poorly. Permission to be a beginner, again, to begin again, anew.

SEARCHING FOR PETCO

For three days, I drive the city in search of Petco.
Day one, I tell myself that Petco will be easy to find.
I don't find Petco.

Day two, I use the GPS feature on my cellphone, but
despite reading the directions before embarking,
I immediately take wrong turn after wrong turn
so naturally it's as if it's a biological need,
like sex or water, to lose myself.

After two hours, I've found rivers and laundromats
and stores of all kinds, but none of them are Petco.
I return home, dejected.

Day three, I arm myself with machete
and research, and I prepare myself for the bush work.
The veins in this city's palms lure me from the bones
into the deep, bloody tissue. I'm a pioneer re-charting

the Mississippi frontier; I'm DaVinci tickling
tendons in corpses, cataloging how the creek
joins the river, how the strip mall scaffolds
the apartment complex. I'm a nursery rhyme,
ringing, the Jersey Ridge bone is connected to the
Utica Ridge bone, and the bones are a body
in which a hundred thousand people respire, inspire,
expire, depending on their mood that day.
I'm in this city's lungs, not at Petco.
In the heart, I spiral around Petco,
but Petco eludes.

For just a jog, a street named Brady is called
Welcome Way. I have a cousin Welcome.
Welcome Normal Lay, she's named.
That's not a diversion, but a reminder to stay
focused, writes Matt Hart in his *Sermons*.
It's so easy to get lost, looking for Petco—
especially when lost, looking for Petco. If in doubt,
take Division, or Locust, or keep going
toward the river, and at the river, start again.

DETOURIST

When the city's never-ending
construction project redirects
traffic away from its shiny,
gentrified facelift, I rediscover
the rust pit of Gaines, of Western,
of Marquette;

Marquette
of my father's house—
old glory, chipped
away with age, chipped up
like teeth, like shoulders bowing.

That house—
owned by an old man
who watched the colonial
mansions recede
into a canopy of trees,
who watched his neighbors disappear
behind blinders as to not see

the wounds of the city
scabbing.

That house
owned by an old man
who died there—
the once grand dining hall converted
to a holding cell, a coffin complete
with a safety shower
and a transplant hospital bed.

Down on Fourth and Gaines,
in front of the Oscar Mayer plant,
the streets besieged
with third-shifters—
    these men too much
    like my father not
    to consider individual—

    these men so old, yet
    still working. Perhaps
    their pensions dried up
    like his; perhaps they too
    have irresponsible poet daughters
    who don't know how to ask

for help until the absolute last
second.

Here, there are children in the street
playing, this small world all theirs.

Here the street is split—
uneven down the middle:
cobblestone & asphalt punctuated
with disrepair. You can't
speed through here
back to that familiar
road; you must go slow
and see the damage
or the damage will take you.

DRIVING RIVER DRIVE EVERY NIGHT FOR THE REST OF MY LIFE

I have never been good at asking for directions.
I would rather watch the moon, the city
reflected in the languid mouth of this
flood-fat river
eroding its way through these
soon-to-change-color trees, these
asphalt streets every spring.

This is a place where I am
a familiar stranger, not my home,
but my homeland. I come like a pilgrim
every summer searching for
those bits of red string I lost

that would make me whole again, if ever
I could find them.

What will my children say
when I too am a part of the road—

my skeleton a stepping stone
for their pitter-pattering feet?

A hundred children will tumble
out of the clown car that is my body,
and they will have red noses
and funny-colored hair; they will direct
traffic in their orange vests and
I will love them like a queen
loves her hive of bees, or
like an everyman loves
but is also simultaneously enslaved by
his own biology.

Here, I am a starved dog
marking my little patches
of land with piss—
just another bespectacled youngin'
in a sea of nondescript tables, trying
to make two and two make more
than logic dictates possible.

CRADLE

on cloudy days
I used to find myself
acting—a case of
overthinking
I used to forge myself
an identity
from these big blue eyes—
expressive, interesting;
at least that's what I told myself

it all seems to boil down
to appearances
when you take all
the living of life
out of the equation;
when I'm older
I wonder if it will
matter less

I'm not sure
whether I should call
it's the weather—
wanting today just to curl up
in the vapid comfort of situational comedies
but knowing
the tasks are piling up
like unwashed dishes—
I miss my myriad idle days
and though I've never been
in a play, here I am
reading lines

PRAYER

Lord give us this day
    our daily breaths
keep us
    from the slaughter
for one more breath
    another
another
    anointed in wonder
wondering after my mother
    and her amaranths—
trying to understand
    this miracle
but always
    coming up short

I'm just a small bird

    yodeling

and hoping

    the yoyoing

won't stop

SATORI

what I'm trying to say is
I'm becoming myself,
and every trip to the river
is a regression
that is becoming harder
and harder to wear

I'm asking for space
to exist, but when I told my mother
I took my vows of refuge
she just said, "great—
now you're going to be mad
about me killing the wasps"
and I said, "Mom,
I've always been
mad about you
killing the wasps"
and there it was:

nothing ever changes
despite the importance we place
on these moments

nobody *is*
despite the mating dances
and the trapper keepers, together
trapped and trapping each other
like rabbits, all of us
canaries with clipped wings

FOOD CHAIN

The current has always been too swift for you, but you insist
on throwing yourself in it headlong, thinking
you're a flat little skipping stone, cute as a button;
you'll skip across these white caps and land
unbruised on the far shore with the fishermen
and their big black boots, but
you're not a skipping stone.

You're a fossil—
veined with primordial ferns,
rough and defined
by the sound of your unladylike plop.

You sink because there is no other way for you.
They say mud becomes you, so you become mud—
and your world becomes a fog
of fish shit, all a-flurry with those microbeads
they can't filter out of the water supply
despite the danger they pose.
You don't know the sky any longer;

you're a bottom feeder—one of those sucker fish,
looking to the light and weeping.
You live on the shit of others,
but you live.

O little blobfish—

you look like you belong when you're deep
in the stink of it, but out in the bright, bright air,
exposed, you're just a boneless mess of flesh
sliming up the boat deck.

O little blobfish—

your body is not accustomed to the world
of air and light, but you must
grow accustomed.

Grow the bones you need
to escape,
the lungs you need
to breathe.

Learn to be the anglerfish
and the angler.

Learn to hold the hopes you carry
like fool's gold around your neck
at arm's length.

Learn to flay
the flesh of those who'd eat of your body.
Fry them up in oil; serve them up crisp.

Remember your logic:
if you cannot skip the seacaps, little blobfish,
and you cannot swim, then you must
hold your breath and walk along the bottom.
Don't worry—It's in your biology
to withstand the pressure cooker
of these depths.

Traditional methods don't apply here, but
the here you're in gives you shape;
it molds you; it guides you in the dark.

This time is the womb from which
you must emerge.

WILSON

To catch a leech, white water raft & crash
onto an Amazonian sandbar, then white water wade
back to shore after your whole soul-searching,
Castaway stint is complete. Reemerge

clear & sinewy. The leeches will flock to your
"whole-new-you" legs, exactly like your old legs,
only sunbaked. If unsuccessful, try again
in all the world's big rivers and laundromats.

Return to your kitchen and spread
your bounty on the cutting board.
Smile; show your teeth as you mince
your prizes and beloveds to paste;
you'll make a pie or pudding.

They will say they love you, but you know
this is not possible. The others will
laugh into their champagne flutes
the next room over, and you will
pray to the volleyball; you will
mince harder.

CHAMPAGNE SABER

I got nothing when the music is easy
& slow / I'm all about the rough patches
& the weep / never the easy sweep of
feel good / I'm so roughrustic / so dropkick
& shudder /
                    I'll try / but I'm a mess / without
my champagne saber / but there's still time
tonight / so belt out a song exploding
you underwhelming miracle / tonight
our veins laced / with champagne /
                                        I have never
danced with a city / I did not love / but
tonight I am not me / I am a body lost
in the fog of bass & treble / & I tremble
before you / my beautiful
Creeping Charlies / at last /
                                    at last / I am

a faceless ghost / funeral shrouded
in sorority black / my eyes half smoke
half glass / I'm a chameleon thrashing
dropping low / leaping high / I am so high
my heart beats at its cage / & I seize
so hard to keep / my brooding a-brooding when
I'm a body in motion /
                                        so let's keep time
tonight / with citrus rinds / put matches
to our tongues / strike oil / strike gold
we're Georgia hot / iron & periodic
mess on the table / I'm all revolution
& quarry when I see you on the edge
of a heartbeat / I'm all skin & earthquake
when you leap

ELEGY FOR SKATE PARK

On the bullet train to who I used to be, I hear a memory
like an MP3 in my ear—a searing snow angel
of speed metal and cowbell.
                        Me, the oxymoron, with my copper
                        intentions laid bare;
you, the pizza arcade of my wonder years, a token
for Funland in a sea
of bicentennial quarters, tied and quartered
between too many hands.
                        We the wolves on the carcass.
                        We the gravity
keeping the birds grounded, scared and intrigued
by the Wild Wild West of the DDR Machine,
the duels decided by the rhythmic
contortions of our adolescent bodies.

We the youthful moshers,
awkwardly composed of Krispy Kreme and mystery
crackers from the back of the pantry, where we
piled into, cramped and silly, every day
for an entire summer.

We all Dance Dance,
We all Revolution,
we all carried away by our Moonlight Shadows
in the roller rink where I, at eleven years old,
heard Three Doors Down's "Kryptonite"
and felt the need to move with such speed I didn't realize
I had wandered face first into a backwards skate.

Yes, they chained me
to the bed with a Ring Pop, a Neopets account, and
nothing else;

Yes, they showered me
with the first silky panties their mothers gave them
in their Easter baskets;

Yes, it was my birthday
and yes, there are pictures and they're just as
embarrassing and uncomfortable
as you're thinking and;
Yes—
Somewhere in the Matrix deathfields of the internet
there is a Neopet named Garlic Stick
that is exactly the days old
that I am from the age of fifteen.
O to be so many years from fifteen now;
O to be the dinosaur Jurassic, no longer
adolescent but surrounded by insurgent youth;
to be *Jurassic Park*; imagined, franchised, then reimagined
and refranchised;
O to be a relic; a reliquary, worshiped
for the penny-thoughts, the fragments
I contain—for my ability to contain holy bodies
O to be a holy body, growing holy bodies;

O holy body

O progeny of red hair

who too may get awkward lingerie from their mother—

O mothers unsure

how to navigate dressing a body with one foot bare,

planted in the mud of childhood

and the other heeled, toe dipped

in discovery, unsure of what comes next—

O world dependent

on dinosaur; on our mother's blood; our bodies adorned

with the black oil of the dead; we American trashcans

full of unfilterable noise—

O world dependent

and doomed.

ALL MY FRIENDS ARE DEAD

love you
friend
like ALL MY FRIENDS ARE DEAD
like I literally live on Friendship St
like I live
in / on / under
the constant duress
of friendship
like friendship looming
friendship glooming
certain city corners

love you
friend
like wrecking ball
like frighteningly large knife collection
like maraca dildoes
like I think I'm gay now
but only for you
like that guy you dragged into bed

on top of me & drunkenly
fumble-fucked
like raccoons in a tree
I am too weak to save
like DROWNING POOL
like LET THE BODIES HIT THE FLOOR
like I wanted to save the wild thing
but the wild thing is doomed
root *dōm*
meaning judgment
meaning glory
but still doomed

love you
friend
like graffiti
like braiding violets
in your hair
like cherry blossoms
all flourish—
fleeting
like hot sake
warm sake
cold sake

like CARD CAPTOR SAKURA
like TAMAGOTCHI
like *otomodatchi*
like supporting character
whose name means friend

love you
friend
like MY LITTLE PONY
like *friendship is magic*
like dead car full of
pot at 3 in the morning
like morning full of
potato scramble

love you
friend
like bacon
like eggs
my soft & greasy friend—
I love you
like forest fire
like THE THINGS THEY CARRIED
like FORGIVENESS, FORGIVENESS

like sledgehammer
like bareknuckle boxing
in a parking lot
like the scary part
of the gym where all
the burly bears are
love you like it hurts
when I pee
when I don't pee
when I drink
when I don't

love you
friend
like Springtime
like APRIL IS THE CRUELEST MONTH

love you
friend
like Ezra loved Eliot
like your poems are fucking difficult, but
I'll make sense of them because I

love you
friend

like APOCALYPSE, PLEASE!
like TWIN TOWERS tower of fire
on the horizon one night
when we were seventeen
like driving forty miles
to the Purina factory
on fire
like holding hands
as ash rained
Pompeii, Pompeii
like CTHULHU
embracing this big
stupid world

love you
friend
like digression
like an adolescence convinced
love was imminent
like imminent disaster
like reading WATCHMEN
and 1984 simultaneously
like this unshakable sensation
we're either spiraling out
into the blackness of

a cold, unrelenting milkyway
or we're waste spiraling
down the drain

in the Andes, now
where you live
it spirals yang to yin
but it's spiraling
still the same
like doom
root *dōm*
meaning glory
meaning judgement
but still doomed

BINARY STAR

Little marble bobbing in a solar pond
        your shifting face all lavarock and lichenmoss—
                                        I love you

As if this envy
        is green and growing—
                                        I love you

As if my spiraling arms of dust and star
        contain the world—
                                        I love you

As if I am a Golden Czar
        doling out forgiveness—
                                        I love you

Down to the lice in your hair

I've named for Roman Gods—

I love you

Down to the very last hair

on your impossible head—

I love you

LINER NOTES

Many of my poems reference other creative works without citing them directly, so I've compiled this list to credit them:

"My Name is Millennial and I'm Not Okay" makes many pop culture allusions, including in-text citations of songs by '80s one-hit-wonders Corey Hart ("I Wear My Sunglasses At Night") and Timbuk 3 ("The Future Is So Bright [I Gotta Wear Shades]").

"Bayonetta" borrows its title and persona from a video game produced by Japanese video game developer PlatinumGames. The poem also makes a reference to Tillie Olsen's short story, "Here I Stand Ironing."

"Rozengurtle Baumgartner, Untouched By Man" quotes several lines from Troy Duffy's original script for *The Boondock Saints*—most of which were cut from the actual film because they didn't test well with audiences.

"Confession" utilizes the catchphrase of popular WWE wrestler Daniel Bryant ("Yes! Yes! Yes!") in its final stanza.

"Making Chloramine Gas in Grandma's Basement" incorporates response to a Surreal Questionnaire, an exercise that generates material from fellow classmates, in a workshop taught by poet Adam Fell.

"Geosmina. Oriol Angrill Jordà, 2012." is an ekphrastic piece written in response to *Geosmina 'The Earth Fragrance,'* a series of blendscapes by Spanish artist Oriol Angrill Jordà first exhibited in 2013.

"Permission" features a quote from "To Shower After Four Days" by Sophia Terezawa, first published in *Poor Claudia*.

"Searching for Petco" borrows a half line from the poem "Amplifier to Defender" by Matt Hart, published in *Sermons and Lectures Both Blank and Relentless.*

"Elegy for Skatepark" changes a half-line from the chorus of DDR classic "Moonlight Shadow" by Missing Heart (itself a cover of Mike Oldfield): "carried away by our Moonlight Shadow."

"All My Friends Are Dead" borrows its title from a book of the same name by Avery Monson and Jory John. Other allusions to creative works In this poem include metalcore band Drowning Pool's "Let the Bodies Hit the Floor"; Japanese manga and anime series *Card Captor Sakura,* developed by CLAMP; kids TV show *My Little Pony* (and their slogan "Friendship is Magic!"), originally developed by toy creator Bonnie Zacherle for Hasbro; Tim O'Brien's *The Things They Carried;* and Shane McCrae's *Forgiveness, Forgiveness.* The first line from T.S. Eliot's "The Wasteland" appears in the sixth stanza. Further on in the poem, there are direct references to Muse's song "Apocalypse, Please!" (from their third studio album, *Absolution),* H.P. Lovecraft's *Call of Chuthulu*, and to J.R.R Tolkien's *The Two Towers*. Final in-text references include Alan Moore's graphic novel *Watchmen* and George Orwell's *1984.*

Two poems in this collection are constructed primarily from found text, borrowed from song titles in my own iTunes library. Listed on the following page, in order of appearance, are the artists whose recordings provided the inspiration—and raw material—for these pieces:

"How Are You Feeling Today" — Bing Crosby • Benny Benassi • Joy Division • Amy Winehouse • Beyoncé • Depeche Mode • Saul Williams • The White Stripes • Amy Winehouse • Smashing Pumpkins • Tom Waits • Pink Floyd • Nirvana • Radiohead • Smashing Pumpkins • Bob Marley & the Wailers • Styx • Bonnie "Prince" Billy • The Pixies • Offenbach • Screamin' Jay Hawkins • Bob Dylan • The Eagles • Stevie Nicks • Sublime • Hole • Sublime • The Sounds • Ray Charles • A Perfect Circle • The Pixies • Andrew Bird • Destiny's Child • Rancid • Pink Floyd • America • Cab Calloway • The Beatles • J. Cole • Muse • Anti-Flag • Aimee Mann • Deathcab for Cutie • Destiny's Child • No Doubt

"Here Comes Your Man" — The Pixies • Roy Brown • Elton John • Cab Calloway & His Orchestra • A Hawk and a Handsaw • David Bowie • Amy Winehouse • The Pixies • The National • Styx • Andrew Bird • Brand New • The Cranberries • t.A.T.u • Clint Mansell • The Shins • Nick Drake • Glen Danzig • Andrew Jackson Jihad • Mariachi El Bronx • Radiohead • Radiohead • The Mountain Goats • The Beatles • The White Stripes • Nine Inch Nails • Murder by Death • Metallica • The Builders and the Butchers • The Shins

ACKNOWLEDGMENTS

The following journals published earlier versions of these poems, some under other titles:

"Mick Foley Death Wish" | *Beholder.* 2019.

"Champagne Saber" | *Beholder.* 2018.

"Satori" | *Mantra.* 2018.

"Cradle" (as "Dear Human Being") | *Forklift, Ohio: A Journal of Poetry, Cooking, & Light Industrial Safety.* 2017.

"The Unicorn" | *Smokelong Quarterly.* 2017.

"Searching for Petco" | *Hobart.* 2016.

"Making Chloramine Gas in Grandma's Basement" (as "On Making Mustard Gas in Grandma's Basement") | *Poetry City, USA.* 2015.

THANKS

A gargantuan thank you to all the friends and family who helped me with this book, especially: my mentor and friend, Ryan Collins; my partner, Sidhartha Roy; and my sister, Cheyenne Taylor.

Immense gratitude to Jennifer Colville at PromptPress, who provided the reading opportunity that led to the publication of this book.

Special shoutout to the Forklift team: Matt Hart, Eric Appleby, and Tricia Suit. Without their support, this book would not have been possible.

Growing up split between an ancestral farmhouse and a busted-up trailer on the banks of the Mississippi River, Skylar Alexander's work centers on pop culture, chronic illness, philosophy, Buddhism, violence, and growing up in rural Iowa. Her writing has appeared in places such as *Cutbank, Smokelong Quarterly, Hobart,* and *Forklift, Ohio.* She studied English and Entrepreneurial Management at the University of Iowa and is pursuing her master's in Education from NYU Steinhardt School of Culture, Education, and Human Development. A former book designer, she now teaches English in the Bronx.

www.skylaralexandermoore.com

Made in the USA
Middletown, DE
21 February 2022

61529013R00068